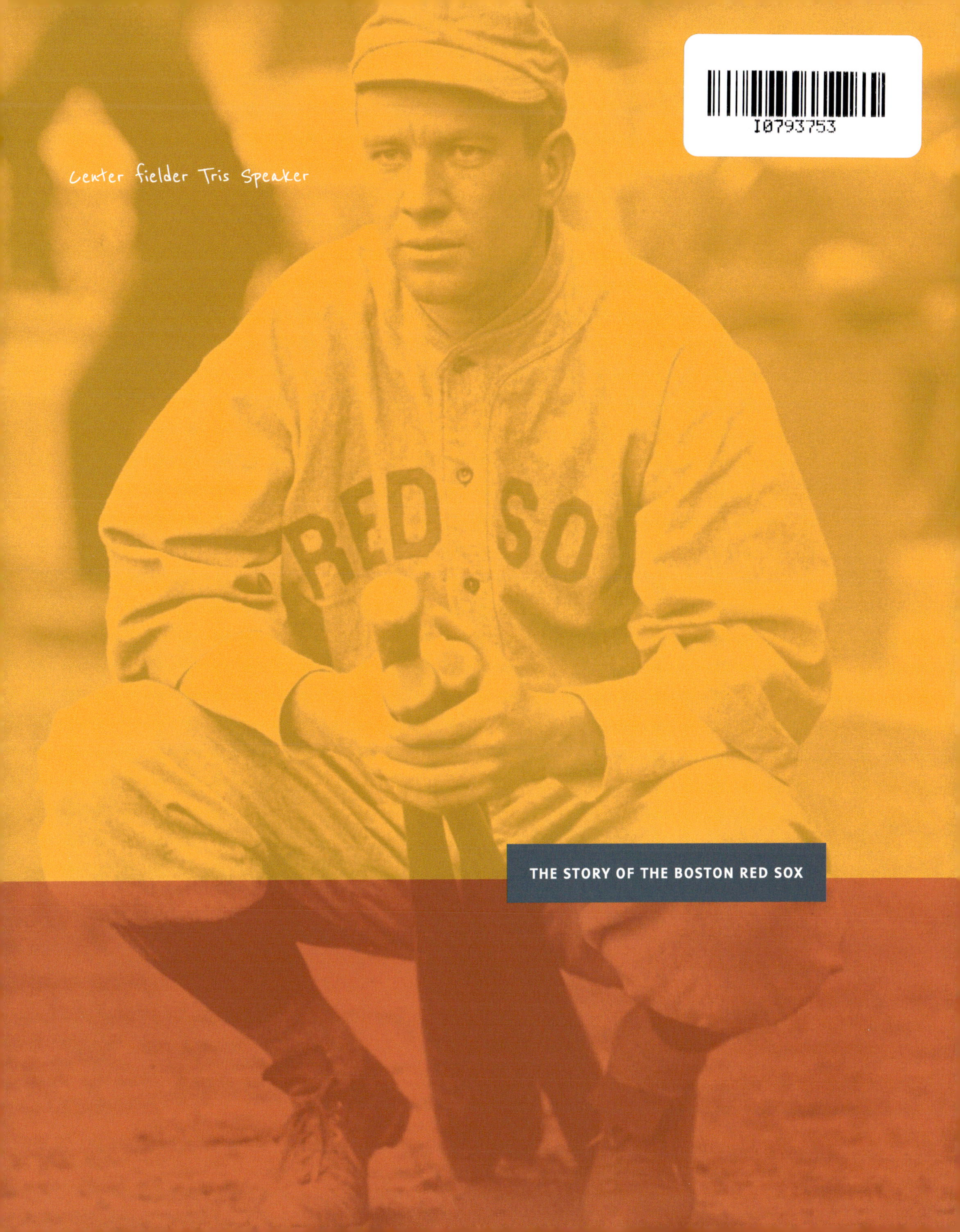

Center fielder Tris Speaker

THE STORY OF THE BOSTON RED SOX

Pitcher Garrett Crochet

THE STORY OF THE

BOSTON RED SOX

JOE TISCHLER

First baseman Adrián González

CREATIVE SPORTS

CREATIVE EDUCATION / CREATIVE PAPERBACKS

Published by Creative Education and Creative Paperbacks
P.O. Box 227, Mankato, Minnesota 56002
Creative Education and Creative Paperbacks are imprints of The Creative Company
www.thecreativecompany.us

Book Design by Wyeth Morgan
Art direction by Blue Design (www.bluedes.com)

Images by Alamy Stock Photo/Nippon News, 29; Getty Images/Al Bello, 11, Brad Mangin, 4–5, 32, Brian Snyder-Pool, 25, Carl Iwasaki, 20, Cooper Neill, 2, 30, Drew Hallowell, 3, Elsa, 6 (bottom, left), Ezra Shaw, 7 (top, right), 10, 26–27, Focus on Sport, 7 (bottom, right), Hulton Archive, 6 (top, left), Jim Davis/The Boston Globe, 22–23, Joseph Scherschel/Time Life Pictures, 7 (top, left), Maddie Meyer, 6 (bottom, right), Matt Stone/MediaNews Group/Boston Herald, cover, Matthew J. Lee/The Boston Globe, 31, National Baseball Hall of Fame Library, 1, 6 (top, right), 12, 14, Rich Pilling, cover, 9, 19, Rick Stewart, 15, Rob Tringali, 7 (bottom, left), Transcendental Graphics, 18; Wikimedia Commons/Los Angeles Daily News/public domain, 16

Library of Congress Cataloging-in-Publication Data
Names: Tischler, Joe author
Title: The story of the Boston Red Sox / Joe Tischler.
Description: Mankato, Mnnesota : Creative Education and Creative Paperbacks, 2026. | Series: Creative sports. Major League Baseball | Includes index. | Audience: Ages 8-12 | Audience: Grades 4-6 | Summary: "Discover the Boston Red Sox's thrilling journey through numerous championship victories, featuring legendary players, iconic moments, and the Major League Baseball team's resilience, culminating in the passionate "Red Sox Nation." Written for middle-grade readers. Includes table of contents, sidebars, and index"– Provided by publisher.
Identifiers: LCCN 2025015974 (print) | LCCN 2025015975 (ebook) | ISBN 9798895810873 library binding | ISBN 9798896800408 paperback | ISBN 9798895812136 ebook
Subjects: LCSH: Boston Red Sox (Baseball team)–History–Juvenile literature
Classification: LCC GV875.B62 T57 2025 (print) | LCC GV875.B62 (ebook) | DDC 796.357/640974461–dc23/eng/20250519
LC record available at https://lccn.loc.gov/2025015974
LC ebook record available at https://lccn.loc.gov/2025015975

Printed in the United States

Pitcher Pedro Martínez

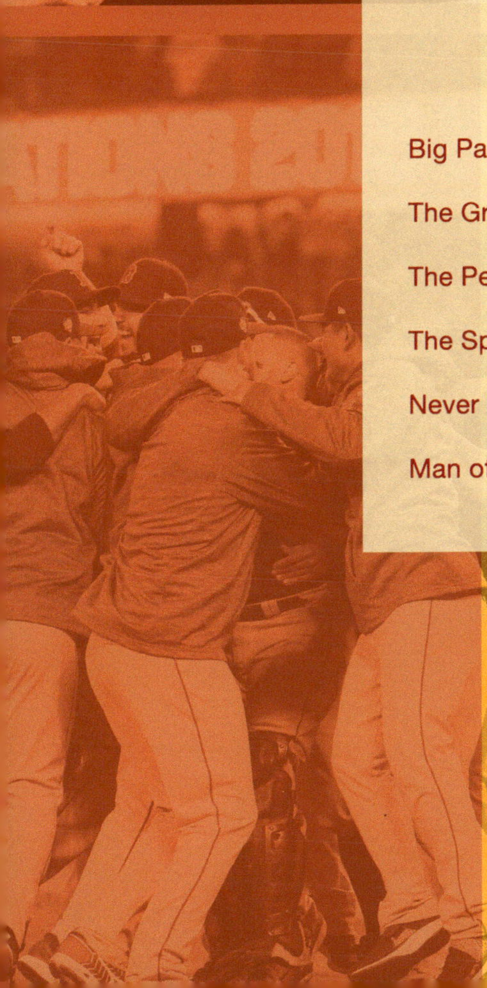

CONTENTS

EXTRA INNINGS

A COMEBACK FOR THE AGES

History was not on the Boston Red Sox's side in the 2004 American League Championship Series (ALCS). The Boston franchise had won five World Series titles, but none since 1918. That was 86 years prior. Meanwhile, their hated rivals, the New York Yankees, had won 26 World Series championships since the Red Sox last won.

The Red Sox were facing the Yankees in this ALCS. New York won the first three games of the best-of-seven series. For the Red Sox to advance to the World Series, they would need to win four straight games. In Major League Baseball (MLB) history, no team had ever come back from a three-games-to-zero deficit to win a series. In Game 4, New York led Boston 4–3 going into the bottom of the ninth inning. Yankees all-star closer Mariano Rivera came in to pitch. Kevin Millar led off for Boston. He drew a walk. Dave Roberts pinch-ran for Millar. Bill Mueller was now at bat. Rivera threw over to first base three times to try to pick off Roberts. He was safe each time. Finally, Rivera threw a pitch to Mueller. Roberts immediately took off for second base. He was safe, just under the tag of Yankees shortstop Derek Jeter. Roberts was now in scoring position. Two pitches later, Mueller

Outfielder Manny Ramírez

EXTRA INNINGS

DAVID ORTIZ
DESIGNATED HITTER
RED SOX SEASONS: 2003–16
HEIGHT: 6-FOOT-3
WEIGHT: 230 POUNDS
KEY STATS: 2022 HALL OF FAME INDUCTEE, 541 CAREER HOME RUNS, 10X ALL-STAR, 2013 WORLD SERIES MVP

BIG PAPI

David Ortiz earned the nickname “Big Papi” for two reasons. One was because of his big size. The other was because he would call people “Papi” if he had trouble remembering their name. He had a postseason to remember in 2004. He hit a game-winning, walk-off home run in an American League Division Series game against the Anaheim Angels. He had his two game-winning walk-off hits in the ALCS against the Yankees. Ortiz had four more hits, including a home run, in the World Series against St. Louis. In 14 postseason games, Ortiz had 22 hits, with five home runs and 19 runs batted in. He is the only player in MLB history to have two walk-off home runs in a single postseason.

Pitcher Curt Schilling during the "Bloody Sock" game

grounded a ball up the middle for a hit and Roberts scored from second to tie the game at 4. The game went into extra innings. Boston was alive. In the bottom of the 12th inning, Manny Ramírez led off with a single. David Ortiz then launched a home run. The Red Sox won 6–4.

Boston still needed three more wins. The next night, the Red Sox trailed again. They scored the tying runs in the eighth inning. Ortiz delivered another walk-off hit, this time in the 14th inning. The Red Sox won 5–4 and now trailed the series three games to two. The series shifted to New York for Game 6 the next night. Boston won that one too, 4–2. This game was known as the "Bloody Sock" game. Red Sox starting pitcher Curt Schilling was playing with a torn tendon in his right ankle. He pitched seven innings and allowed just one run. Blood could be seen on Schilling's sock throughout the game. The Red Sox were now one game away from making baseball history.

Boston had momentum on their side for Game 7. Ortiz hit a two-run home run in the top of the first inning. They loaded the bases in the top of the second inning. Johnny Damon brought them all home with a grand slam over the right field wall. They led 6–0. The Red Sox went on to win 10–3 and complete the greatest series comeback in MLB history. The St. Louis Cardinals were no match for the Red Sox in the World Series. Boston swept St. Louis in four games. The Red Sox were World Series champions for the first time in 86 years!

CY AND THE CURSE

The success of the 2004 season echoed how the franchise began in 1901. Boston was a charter member of the American League (AL). The team was first officially known as the Americans. Some referred to them as the Pilgrims.

Boston played in baseball's first World Series in 1903. The Americans won the AL pennant. They took on the National League (NL) champion Pittsburgh Pirates. Boston lost three of the first four games of the best-of-nine series. They won the next four and claimed MLB's first world championship. Boston won the AL pennant the following year, too. But no World Series was held. The NL champion, the New York Giants, did not want to play the champion of the inferior AL.

Pitcher Cy Young led the AL with 28 wins in 1903. He was one of baseball's first premier pitchers. His career started in 1890 and lasted for 22 years. He holds several major-league records, including career wins (511), games started (815), and innings pitched (7,356). Today, baseball honors the best pitcher in each league with the Cy Young Award.

Before the 1908 season, the Boston franchise changed its name. Team owner John I. Taylor changed the team's stockings to red. The team became known as the Red Sox. Taylor traded away many of Boston's best players, replacing them with younger, cheaper talent. Some of the money he saved helped build a new stadium. A new ballpark called Fenway Park opened in 1912. It is well-noted for its 37-foot-high fence in left field. It is known as the "Green Monster." The Red Sox still play there today. It is MLB's oldest ballpark.

Pitcher Cy Young

Several of the young players Taylor signed became stars. The Red Sox were on their way to becoming winners again. They won the AL pennant in 1912. "Smoky Joe" Wood fired pitches across the plate. Outfielder Tris Speaker was one of baseball's best hitters. Wood won 34 games on the mound. Speaker hit .383 and stole 52 bases. He was named AL's Most Valuable Player (MVP). In a best-of-seven World Series, the Red Sox defeated the Giants in seven games. Boston claimed its second world championship.

Pitcher George Herman "Babe" Ruth

Two years later, the Red Sox signed a young pitcher named George Herman "Babe" Ruth. "The Bambino" won 18 games in his first full season in 1915. The Red Sox won their third World Series title. They beat the Philadelphia Phillies. Boston won again the following year. Ruth did even better on the mound, winning 23 games. Ruth could also hit the ball hard and far. When he wasn't pitching, he would play outfield. He led MLB in home runs for the first time in 1918. Boston won another World Series title that year. They beat the Chicago Cubs in six games.

Harry Frazee now owned the team. He refused to give Ruth the raise he wanted. Instead, Frazee sold him to the rival New York Yankees after the 1919 season. According to popular legend, the Ruth sale put a curse on the team. The "Curse of the Bambino" seemed to have an immediate effect. Boston posted losing records for the next 14 years. The Curse haunted the team for decades.

EXTRA INNINGS

THE GREEN MONSTER

Fenway Park opened in 1912. In left field is a wall that stands 37-feet, 2-inches high. It is the highest wall in Major League Baseball. It is called the "Green Monster." The Green Monster was not painted green until 1947. Advertisements covered the wall before then. Sitting just 310 feet down the left field line, the wall is a hitting haven for right-handed batters. Batted balls are routinely smacked off the wall. A net was installed in 1936 over the wall to help keep home run balls from hitting nearby businesses. It was removed in 2003. Ownership added rows of seating for fans. These "Monster seats" are some of the most sought-after places to watch a game in all of baseball.

EXTRA INNINGS

JOHNNY PESKY
1946 WORLD SERIES

JOHNNY PESKY
INFIELDER
RED SOX SEASONS: 1942, 1946–52
HEIGHT: 5-FOOT-9
WEIGHT: 168 POUNDS
KEY STATS: 1946 ALL-STAR, 3X AL HITS LEADER, 1,455 CAREER HITS, .307 CAREER BATTING AVERAGE

THE PESKY POLE

Johnny Pesky's lifetime .307 batting average is a testament to his hitting skill. But during his time with the Red Sox, Pesky slugged just 13 home runs. Six came at Fenway Park. Pesky's Fenway homers barely slipped over the 3-foot-high right-field fence next to the foul pole. That is just 302 feet away from home plate. It is the shortest distance for a home run in the major leagues. Pesky's Boston teammate Mel Parnell jokingly called the right-field foul pole the "Pesky Pole." The nickname stuck. In 2006, the Red Sox officially named the yellow marker the Pesky Pole.

PRECISION HITTERS

In 1933, shortly after his 30th birthday, Tom Yawkey purchased the struggling Red Sox. Yawkey's passion was baseball. He wanted to build a winning team. He signed top players like slugging first baseman Jimmie Foxx and strikeout king Lefty Grove. Yawkey also built up the team's minor-league system. It soon produced steady-hitting second baseman Bobby Doerr and outfielder Ted Williams.

The lanky and slender Williams came up to the major leagues in 1939. He did not look like much. But his outstanding play quickly earned him the nickname "The Splendid Splinter." He once said, "All I want out of life is that when I walk down the street, folks will say, 'there goes the greatest hitter who ever lived.'" Many experts agree that he is.

The team showed modest improvement under Yawkey's ownership. It had seven winning seasons in the next 13 years. In the early 1940s, many MLB players served in World War II, including Williams. After the war ended, they returned. Boston won 104 games in 1946. It took its first AL pennant in 28 years. Boston's lineup included swift center fielder Dom DiMaggio and infielder Johnny Pesky. In the World Series, the Red Sox faced the St. Louis Cardinals. St. Louis won the series in seven games. Some people saw the infamous Curse at work.

The Red Sox did not reach the playoffs again for more than two decades. Williams retired in 1960. Another power-hitting outfielder arrived the following year: Carl "Yaz" Yastrzemski. He said, "I knew there was only one Ted Williams, but I was going to give them everything Carl Yastrzemski had." That confident attitude helped Yaz win three AL batting titles.

Outfielder Ted William

Boston continued to struggle through the mid-1960s. Then, in 1967, the team caught fire. Fueled by Yaz's Triple Crown season, it rocketed to the top of the league. A batting Triple Crown consists of leading the league in batting average, home runs, and runs batted in. The Red Sox met the Cardinals again in the World Series. Again, they lost to them in seven games.

In 1969, MLB split each league into two divisions. Six years later, the Red Sox stormed to their first AL East Division title. Boston had bolstered its lineup with young stars. They included catcher Carlton Fisk and multi-talented outfielders Jim Rice, Fred Lynn, and Dwight Evans. The Red Sox swept the Oakland Athletics in the ALCS. They met the Cincinnati Reds in the World Series. Game 6 was historic. In the bottom of the 12th inning, Fisk hit a blast down the left field line. He frantically waved his arms in hopes the ball would remain fair over the Green Monster. It did. The Red Sox won 7–6. Cincinnati won the following night to win the series.

Outfielder Dwight Evans

TED WILLIAMS
LEFT FIELDER
RED SOX SEASONS: 1939–42, 1946–60
HEIGHT: 6-FOOT-3
WEIGHT: 205 POUNDS
KEY STATS: 1966 HALL OF FAME INDUCTEE, 521 CAREER HOME RUNS, 19X ALL-STAR, 2X AL MVP, 6X BATTING TITLE

THE SPLENDID SPLINTER

Ted Williams was a great hitter the moment he first stepped onto a baseball diamond. He batted .327 in his first season with the Boston Red Sox in 1939. He raised that mark to .344 the following season. In 1941, he was flirting with history with a .400 batting average. Only seven other AL/NL players had achieved the feat in the 20th century. Williams was right at .400 on the final day of the season. Boston had a doubleheader scheduled. He could have sat. But he didn't. Williams had six hits on the day and his final average rose to .406. The closest AL/NL player to achieve that feat since is Tony Gwynn. He batted .394 in the strike-shortened 1994 season.

ENDING THE CURSE

In 1978, Boston and New York tied for the AL East title. The teams faced off in a one-game tiebreaker to decide the division winner. In the seventh inning, light-hitting Yankees shortstop Bucky Dent hit a fly over the Green Monster. It was a three-run home run. The Yankees won 5–4. The Curse had struck again.

Yastrzemski retired in 1983. He spent his entire 23-year career with Boston. By the mid-1980s, a new group of stars was shining in Fenway Park. Third baseman Wade Boggs was a hitting machine. He captured five AL batting titles. "Rocket" Roger Clemens was a power-pitching ace. He holds the major-league record for strikeouts in a game with 20. He did it twice.

In 1986, Clemens won 24 games. Boggs hit .357. Boston took the AL East. The Red Sox advanced to the World Series. They faced the New York Mets. Boston led the series three games to two. In Game 6, it held a 5–3 lead with two outs in the bottom of the 10th inning. The Mets hit three straight singles. The tying run scored on a wild pitch. Then first baseman Bill Buckner made a fielding error. That allowed the winning run to score. To Boston fans, this proved the Curse was still alive. The Mets won Game 7 and won the series.

The Red Sox remained a contender for the next few years. Then they went into a downward spin. Boston suffered losing records from 1992 to 1994. It bounced back in 1995. Burly first baseman Mo Vaughn smashed 39 home runs and drove in 126 runs. He was named AL Most Valuable Player. The Red Sox won their division. But they fell short of the World Series.

By 2003, Boston had several strong core players. Outfielder Manny Ramírez slugged 37 home runs. Shortstop Nomar Garciaparra added 28. Pedro Martínez

Pitcher Pedro Martínez

owned the pitcher's mound. He won two AL Cy Young Awards while pitching for Boston (1999, 2000). The team made the postseason. But the Curse struck yet again. In Game 7 of the ALCS against the Yankees, Aaron Boone hit a walk-off home run in the 11th inning. The Yankees advanced to the World Series. The moment reminded fans of Bucky Dent's 1978 home run.

Boston welcomed a new pitching star in 2004. Righthander Curt Schilling brought World Series experience. He won a title with the Arizona Diamondbacks in 2001. Ramírez and designated hitter David Ortiz combined for 84 home runs. Boston reached the playoffs again. It defeated the Anaheim Angels in the Division Series. Then the Red Sox faced the Yankees again in the ALCS. Boston staged the miraculous comeback from a 3–0 deficit to win the series in seven games. In the World Series, the Red Sox faced the Cardinals. Boston crushed them in four games. It captured its first world championship since 1918. The Curse was over! "This [victory] is for Ted Williams, Yaz, and all the other great players who made this franchise what it is today," said Schilling. "We are all proud to wear this uniform."

MORE TITLES

Fans had waited 86 years to celebrate a World Series victory. They only had to wait three years for the next one. In 2007, Boston featured a strong trio of pitchers. Hard-throwing Josh Beckett, knuckleballer Tim Wakefield, and closer Jonathan Papelbon took turns on the mound. The Red Sox also had

Designated hitter David Ortiz with Johnny Pesky

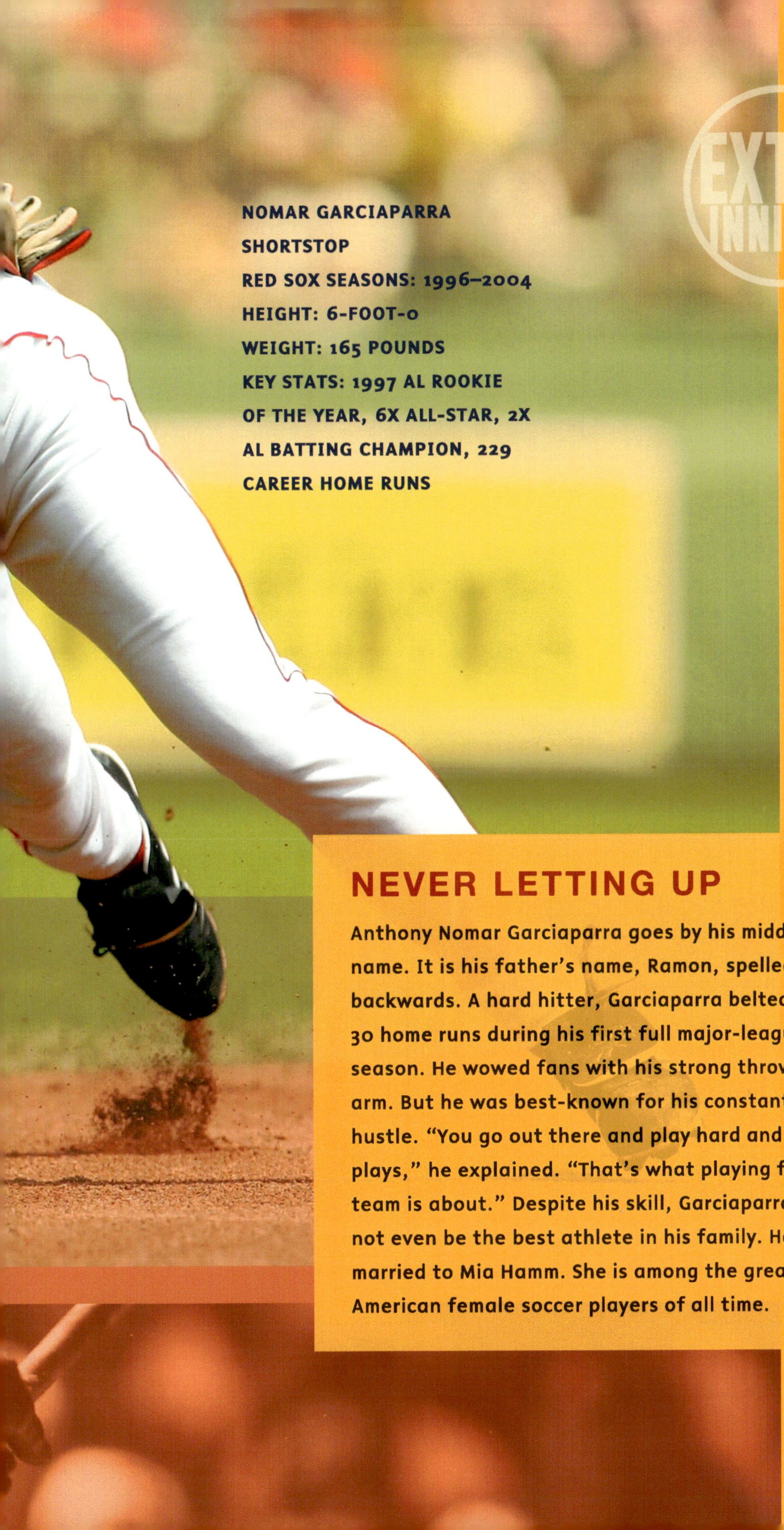

EXTRA INNINGS

NOMAR GARCIAPARRA
SHORTSTOP
RED SOX SEASONS: 1996–2004
HEIGHT: 6-FOOT-0
WEIGHT: 165 POUNDS
KEY STATS: 1997 AL ROOKIE OF THE YEAR, 6X ALL-STAR, 2X AL BATTING CHAMPION, 229 CAREER HOME RUNS

NEVER LETTING UP

Anthony Nomar Garciaparra goes by his middle name. It is his father's name, Ramon, spelled backwards. A hard hitter, Garciaparra belted 30 home runs during his first full major-league season. He wowed fans with his strong throwing arm. But he was best-known for his constant hustle. "You go out there and play hard and make plays," he explained. "That's what playing for this team is about." Despite his skill, Garciaparra may not even be the best athlete in his family. He is married to Mia Hamm. She is among the greatest American female soccer players of all time.

two promising rookies in gritty second baseman Dustin Pedroia and speedy outfielder Jacoby Ellsbury. Boston swept the Colorado Rockies in four games in the World Series. Third baseman Mike Lowell was named series MVP. He batted .400 against Colorado.

The Red Sox returned to the playoffs the following two seasons. They fell just short of returning to the World Series in 2008. They fell to the Tampa Bay Rays in the ALCS in seven games. The team then lost to the Los Angeles Angels of Anaheim in the Division Series the following season.

Boston failed to qualify for the playoffs the following three seasons. That included a 93-loss, last-place finish in 2012. The next year, the Red Sox were back on top. They won 97 games and won the division. Boston defeated Tampa Bay and the Detroit Tigers in the AL playoffs. They were back in the World Series. A familiar opponent faced them, the St. Louis Cardinals. Boston won in six games. Ortiz had a remarkable series. He batted .688 in the series with 11 hits and 2 home runs. He was the easy choice for series MVP.

The Red Sox couldn't keep the momentum the next two years. They had losing records both seasons. Boston returned to the postseason in 2016 and 2017. But it lost in the Division Series both years.

The 2018 season was historic. Boston amassed a franchise-best 108 wins. Outfielder Mookie Betts established himself as one of the elite players in the game. He was named AL MVP after leading the league in batting at .346. The team cruised through the AL playoffs defeating the Yankees and Houston Astros. It lost only one game in each series. The Red Sox faced the Los Angeles Dodgers in the World Series. They won the series in five games. It was their ninth title and fourth over a 15-year span.

MOOKIE BETTS
OUTFIELDER
RED SOX SEASONS: 2014–19
HEIGHT: 5-FOOT-9
WEIGHT: 180 POUNDS
KEY STATS: 2018 AL MVP, 8X ALL-STAR, 6X GOLD GLOVE WINNER, 7X SILVER SLUGGER WINNER

EXTRA INNINGS

MAN OF MANY FIRSTS

In 2018, Mookie Betts made history. He became the first player to win the MVP, Silver Slugger, Gold Glove, batting title, and World Series in the same season. He also led the majors in runs scored. Earlier in the season, Betts became the youngest player to have four three-homer games. He excels in another sport, too. "Bowling has been a part of my life forever," he said. He is the first Professional Bowlers Association (PBA) member to win a World Series. He rolled a perfect 300 game in the PBA World Series of Bowling in 2017. He also may be the first MLB player related to a member of the British royal family. He is a distant cousin of former actress Meghan Markle, who married Prince Harry in 2018.

MassMutual

Third baseman Rafael Devers

Boston failed to make the playoffs in 2019. The COVID-19 pandemic cut the 2020 season short. The season was halted during spring training in March. The season restarted in late July and was shortened to 60 games. The Red Sox finished just 24–36.

The Red Sox won 92 games in 2021. They defeated division foes New York and Tampa Bay on their way to the ALCS. Boston fell to Houston in six games. The team had identical 78–84 records the next two seasons. It missed the postseason. The Red Sox improved to 81 wins in 2024. Again, they fell short of the playoffs.

The Boston Red Sox have given their fans a colorful history. Their story is filled with championship victories, heartbreaking defeats, a curse, and even a green monster. The team looks to consistently get back in the postseason with young hitting stars like outfielder Jarren Duran and third baseman Rafael Devers. Sports fans throughout New England proudly proclaim themselves citizens of "Red Sox Nation."

Outfielder Jarren Duran

INDEX